How to Stick With Your Budget

129 Proven Ways to Spend Less and Save

More Money this Month

By Tracy Chitwood

About the author

Tracy Chitwood, the author of this helpful guide to sticking to a budget has a deep passion for personal finance.

She is an experienced professional who likes to break down budgeting and money management into simple, and actionable steps.

As a certified financial planner, Chitwood has been dedicated to helping individuals take back control of their finances and build lasting wealth for 15 years.

In addition to writing, Chitwood is a motivational speaker and a teacher. She inspires youths to avoid making the same financial mistakes many parents made.

In "How to Stick to Your Budget, 129 Proven Ways to Spend Less and Save More Money this Month" she shares proven secrets to managing your money much better.

Discover more habits you need to embrace to stay on budget.

Table of Contents

Introduction

Creating a budget doesn't imply that you won't be able to enjoy yourself or be limited. In actuality, it's the complete opposite. You can enjoy yourself without feeling guilty. All a budget does is to specify where your money should go. The budget by itself poses no threat. Most people discover that they feel like they got a raise after adhering to their first budget! I felt the same way too.

Before we get into our main topic, let's take a look at a few reasons why you should stick to a budget that was put together by you for you.

- Maintaining your budget stops overspending
- Adhering to your budget exposes unhealthy spending patterns
- A budget assists in preparing for emergencies.
- Having a budget aids you to reach long- term targets. It might be paying off the mortgage more quickly or retiring early.
- Abiding by your budget facilitates retirement saving
- Setting a budget allows you to proactively manage, reduce, and eliminate debt.

Sticking to a budget can be difficult, but there are creative strategies that can make the process more enjoyable and sustainable. Now let's discover creative ways to stay within your budget.

Part One

1. **Make the financial goals you have noticeable**

   Give yourself reasons for the sacrifices you will make. Keep a visible reminder of your goals close at hand. It might be a picture of your ideal home or vehicle, or a vision board. I recommend you use my *"Financial Freedom Goal Monthly Budget Planner: Go from Broke to Wealthy with the Power of 7"* on Amazon to help you progress better on this journey.

1. **List your sources of income, together with the monthly, weekly, or yearly amounts that you generate**

2. **Make a list of all your expenditures and their budgeted amounts, and rank them in order of significance**

   For example, food, housing, and transportation ought to be at the top of your list. Lay out funds for them in that order. Sometimes you'd discover that you can do without some. Keep your total expenditures below your earnings.

3. Break your financial objectives into small steps

For instance, you could consider putting aside $100 a week if you have to budget $400 per month for school expenses the following year. This will assist you in staying on track, particularly if you are new to budgeting.

4. Have a list of your wants versus needs

Listing your needs and wants helps you distinguish between the two. Spend money on needs first and delay purchasing your wants.

5. Pay yourself first and keep some money for pleasure.

If your budget is so tight that you are unable to enjoy yourself at all, you will not be able to abide by it.

6. Start Small

You are unlikely to stick with a budget of 1 coffee per day if you buy 5 per day now. Lower it to 4 at first, and then to less as you make good progress. It's not so much about the big things you do, but rather the small ones.

7. **Be realistic about budgeted amounts**

    When you sit down to plan your categories, keep a realistic mindset. For instance, it's easier to complete a one-month challenge to eat out less than it is to reduce your family's monthly grocery expenditure from $800 to $200 for four people.

8. **Educate yourself on budgeting**

    Go through as many books and blog posts as you can on budgeting. Check out videos and podcasts about money. They'll assist you in altering and improving your financial mindset, which includes your attitude and convictions about money.

9. **Make deductions in areas that impact the entire family**

Make sure you are in it together if you want to keep your family together.

10. Act as though you only have the monthly amount you allocated

Probably the most difficult step is to pretend that you have nothing but your allowance each month.

11. Use the Cash Envelope Budget System

Allocate specified amounts of cash to various categories of spending and physically separating the funds with envelopes. You're done with that category of spending until the next month when the envelope is empty.

12. Follow the 24 hours to 30 days rule

Wait for twenty-four hours or more before making any non-essential purchases or payments that aren't on your list of expenses. Think about the potential value of that money for you in the future. Ask yourself if you really need the item or service. Can you make use of something else? Is it possible for it to wait? This reduces impulsive purchases.

13. Have an accountability partner

If your spouse isn't available or you don't have one, tell a trusted friend about your plans. You could rely on them for support.

15. Become familiar with the criticism from friends and family regarding your decision

Not everyone will agree with the choices you make. There will be remarks when you are unable to do something. Tell them when it's not in the budget and try not to let it bother you.

16. Review and make changes

Check your expenditures at the end of each month to ensure that you have lived comfortably and haven't overspent.

17. Celebrate financial achievements

Acknowledge your financial accomplishments. When you reach your savings targets, treat yourself in small, affordable ways.

18. Change the bank account you use

You might think about moving to a bank or account type that offers you interest or charges less if your present bank account has fees.

19. If you have a credit score, raise it

20. Avoid using credit cards

To avoid going over budget, bring just enough cash to the store. Don't increase your debt in subsequent budgets. Use a debit card instead if you have to, or don't buy anything if you can't pay with cash.

21. Prioritize paying off high-interest debt

It makes sense to pay off debts that accrue interest quickly first, such as credit card debt. By doing so you end up paying less interest overall.

22. Live a month behind AND pay your bills one month in advance

Although this is a crucial step, it is perhaps the hardest. Use the money you earn this month to pay for your living expenses for the next month. In this manner, you won't have to worry about when your bills and paychecks are due. Almost always, you would have some extra money to save. If you were to lose your job, you could also adjust more readily.

23. **Create an expense-free challenge schedule**
Choose days, weekends, or even entire months that you will limit your spending to necessities. You could take part in no-spend challenges with friends or try a no-new-clothe challenge.

24. **Avoid saving your credit/debit card numbers on your phone, computer or internet retailers' websites**

25. **Be mindful of concealed fees, like ATM withdrawal fees**

26. **Make use of reward or cash-back apps that compensate you for regular purchases**

Get reimbursed for gas, groceries, and internet purchases.

27. When you go out occasionally, leave your wallet at home or at office

28. Do not spend loose change.

Make a jar or box to save them. You can use an image of your savings target to decorate it. Put spare change into it on a regular basis. You can deposit the money into a savings account once the jar is full.

29. Put Away Extra Cash

Congratulations on achieving your much-needed bonus. It would be best to put extra cash like bonuses and tips in your savings account. Keep it hidden from view, or alternately, use it to settle some of your debt.

30. Automate Bill Payments and Savings

Handle your savings as though they were a bill that needs to be paid. Set up automatic transfers to your savings account.

An excellent way to remember to make some payments even when you forget is to set up auto draft. Bills can be automatically paid with this option.

31. Set up all your insurance plans with one service provider

It's easier to get discounts on two or more policies if you do so.

32. Get your tax refund

A student that is put on an emergency taxx code by an employer may be entitled to a tax refund. The owner of a student business may also lay some claims and have less profits taxed.

33. Enrol in an assistance program

You may receive food assistance from the Supplemental Nutrition Assistance Program (SNAP), also known as food stamps.

Utility and rent expenses can be subsidized by the Low Income Home Energy Assistance

Program (LIHEAP), and the Section 8 Housing Choice Voucher Program respectively.

Eligibility for these programs depends on income and family size.

Medical assistance programs such as Medicaid provide Health insurance to low-income residents, children, pregnant women, and people with disabilities.

The Federal Pell Grant provides financial aid for college tuition and other educational expenses. Eligibility varies with income too, so it is important to check whether you are eligible.

Apply for such programs online through the program's website or visit your local social services office to do so.

PART TWO

HEALTH

34. Continue living a healthful lifestyle

Maintain your health and cut costs on prescription drugs, doctor visits, and other medical bills by engaging in physical activity and eating a well-balanced diet.

35. Suspend supplements

Eat nutritious foods instead.

36. Benefit from free screenings

37. Survey the prices of laboratory tests in various institutions first.

38. Pay attention to your doctor's advice.

Failure to do so may result in additional medical expenses.

39. Take telemedicine into consideration

40.   **Get a second opinion whenever the doctor suggests costly procedures**

41.   **Purchasing only name-brand medications is not cost-effective**

Despite a price difference, a drug's effect will remain the same as long as the active ingredient and its quantity are the same. But just in case, be sure to look over the inactive ingredients as well if you have any allergies.

42.   **Exercise at home**

You don't need to go to the gym to work out because there are plenty of free online workout resources. Pair with a friend and hold each other accountable if you need motivation. Gym memberships can be expensive.

UTILITIES

43. **Debate about bills and subscriptions**

Examine your subscription services and utility bills on a regular basis. To get better prices, haggle with your suppliers, and cancel any subscriptions you are not using.

44. **Take advantage of free trials of streaming services and explore different options before choosing a paid subscription.**

45. **Downgrade your cell phone plan if you're on a low income to one that still has enough talk time and data to meet your monthly needs**

46. **Unplug unused appliances and turn off the lights when you're not using them.**

This will result in monthly energy bill savings.

47. **Install a programmable thermostat**

One that can be adjusted to a lower temperature when no one is home or sleeping.

48. **Electric blankets are a great way to keep warm and save money on energy bills.**

They cost much less than installing a radiator.

49. **Install storm windows, caulk windows and doors, and add insulation to your home to make it winter-ready.**

These will lower heating expenses and help retain heat during the winter.

50. **Make use of natural light and ventilation instead of using artificial lighting and air conditioning.**

It's a fantastic method to maintain your health and save energy.

52. **Hang laundry to dry instead of using a dryer**

53. **Take showers rather than baths**

While you are scrubbing, you might also try setting a timer and turning off the water.

53. **Collect rainwater for home and gardening uses**

Rainwater is free and useful for a variety of home and gardening purposes.

54. **Sign up for a time-of-use plan with your energy provider**

Many local energy providers offer discounts to reduce your electricity consumption during peak hours. This includes washing your clothes and dishes during off-peak hours at night.

55. **Install a dimmer switch and use energy efficient halogen bulbs instead of incandescent bulbs**

56. **You don't have to pay for heating and cooling unused rooms. Keep them closed.**

Entertainment

57.   Visit eateries where children eat for free

58.   Instead of choosing dinner, go out for lunch or during happy hour.

Then, it usually costs less.

59.   Enjoy free online resources like podcasts and YouTube videos

60.   Check out free recreational options

Find free or inexpensive entertainment options in your neighbourhood, such as plays and outdoor events.

61.   Visit movie theatres at off-peak times, or spend more time on YouTube

Although weekends and evenings seem like the ideal times to see a movie, these are also the times when movie theatres are known to raise their ticket prices. If you go to the movies Monday through Thursday before 5 p.m., you'll often save a good amount of money.

62. **Organize budget-friendly events**

Organize low-cost events at your house or in public areas rather than paying for fancy venues. You can socialize without going over budget in this way.

63. **Explore and develop creative interests that do not require expensive materials or equipment**

Painting, writing, and singing can be done without the need of expensive materials or equipment. They provide great fun and self-expression. You can also try dancing to some good music.

FOOD AND DRINKS

64. Prepare at least 85% of your meals at home
Utilize what is in your pantry. Stock up on less expensive food. Snacks from home are far tastier than junk food from the store. They frequently have fewer additives, are healthier, and cost less.

65. Set up a personal or community or garden
Joining a community garden to cultivate your own fruits and vegetables is an affordable way to save money and enjoy fresh produce if you can't have your own.

66. Prepare lunch beforehand and carry it along

67. Become a member of a food cooperative
If you're fortunate enough to reside in a place where a Food Co-Op is present, make use of the opportunity. They typically offer mixed food produce at a lesser price than grocery stores which are delivered to a central pick-up point.

68. Purchase less red meat

Pork is more expensive than chicken, but beef is more expensive still. When you're on a tight budget, your meals ought to be organized around the less expensive meats.

69. Reduce the amount of meat used in meals

Add more vegetables, lentils, oats and beans. This can help reduce the cost of a meal.

70. Don't throw away leftover meals - turn them into a new meal

71. Reduce your soda consumption

Make it a weekend treat or a special occasion because it costs more than water.

72. Ignore fruit juice.

Eat some fruits instead of drinking fruit juice. Fruit juice is costly, and if consumed frequently is bad for your teeth.

73. Replace bottled water

In the west, purchasing drinking water is really not necessary because our drinking-water is generally safe. Invest in a water filter jug if the taste of your tap water is foul. To ensure you always have cold water to take along, keep filled reusable water bottles in the fridge.

74. Reduce your alcohol consumption

Alcohol is costly, and many governments tax it heavily on top of its base cost.

75. Brewing your coffee at home instead of buying it at the store is a cost-effective option.

76. Instead of purchasing baby food, prepare your own

Making baby food at home can be an inexpensive and wholesome substitute to store-bought infant formula. It allows you to keep an eye on the ingredients and make sure your baby is getting the best nutrition possible.

SHOPPING TIPS

77. Stay clear of compulsive shoppers and your spending triggers

Spend as little time as possible with friends who seem to spend money everywhere they go or who love to shop. Avoid lingering in stores and shopping centres. Take an alternate route rather than the one that goes by the shop you love.

78. Pick up orders in person rather than have them delivered

79. Reduce the frequency of your shopping trips

Try to stretch out your shopping to once a week or longer.

80. Go shopping alone

Take neither your spouse nor the children. Usually, you would have to pay more if they went.

81. **Do not shop when your stomach Is empty**

Everything appears more appetizing and your brain tells you to buy more food when you're hungry. This is not ideal if you want to cut back on how much you spend on shopping.

82. **Carry snacks with you when you go on long errands**

83. **Compare brands before you shop for products**

When compared to name brands, other brands frequently offer the same quality at a lower price.

84. **Try your local farmers' market and shop at several different stores**

Certain markets can be excellent places to find inexpensive produce, particularly in the latter hours of the day when vendors are attempting to clear out their remaining inventory.

85. **Shop during specific hours of the day**

Generally speaking, buying groceries late at night is not the best option. Frequently, the most affordable items may be sold out, forcing you to purchase the more costly model. In addition, you might be extremely exhausted at that point and inclined to make rash choices in an effort to finish your shopping and head home. Aim to shop during off-peak hours. Being in a crowd can make you feel more stressed and less able to reason perfectly.

86. Invest in bulk purchases sometimes

Purchasing in bulk can result in a more favourable price than buying a packet of a more standard size. However, this is not always the case. To be sure you are truly getting a good deal, always check the unit price of the bulk items.

The amount of the bulk-purchased item that you actually eat must also be taken into account. You might eat pasta and rice on a regular basis, but maybe not cans of beans. When purchasing meat, for example, buy in bulk because you know you'll use it frequently and it can be stored safely for a long time. Rather than purchasing single serving and snack packs, opt for the larger, cheaper option. They can be divided into separate servings and containers afterwards.

87.   Budget your gifts for special occasions

For instance, you may decide to spend a maximum of $50 for adults, $20 for children aged 7 to 18, and $15 on gifts for friends and family under the age of seven.

88.   Be careful of promotions like "buy one, get one free"

They are almost always found on luxurious brands of goods rather than discount store brands. Part of the reasons why premium brands are more expensive is that the producers have to make up for all the money they have invested in advertising to convince us that their product is the best. Do your calculations well.

89. **Shop with coupons to save money on groceries, clothing, toiletries and other household items.**

90. **Go with and adhere to your list**
Become an expert at creating and adhering to your shopping or to-do list.

91. **Don't buy items you "might need one day" until you need them**

92. **Purchase products and food in season**
When buying goods and food, think about what's in season and what's not. For example, firewood is cheaper in the spring than in winter.

93. **Paying more for a higher quality items may be wiser**
A $100 pair of shoes that lasts for six years is ultimately a better buy than a $20 pair of shoes that only lasts one year.

94. **Consider second-hand stores for apparel, furnishings, and home goods.**

Unique items can be found for a much lower price than brand-new ones at such places.

95.   Buy reusable items such as cloth napkins and bags and save the environment too.

TRANSPORTATION AND TRAVEL

96. **Walk short distances, take taxis, or use public transport instead of driving**

Although it's not always convenient, you'll save money on repairs and insurance, as well as the cost of a car itself.

97. **Make fewer trips**

With more careful planning and a few strategies, you can batch errands together and save both time and gas money.

98. **Adhere to traffic rules and avoid fines**

99. **Avoid paying for parking spaces**

100. **Do not move around with an empty or full fuel tank**

It sounds strange that you shouldn't fill up your tank with gas, but it adds weight to your car. This means the engine has to work harder (and use more gas) to keep moving. Moving with just a little fuel in the tank on a regular basis can damage your engine. Try to keep the fuel gauge between a half and three- quarters full.

101. Rotate the tires and ensure that they are properly inflated

A car's wheels bear the loads of driving in diverse ways. The front wheels bear the brakes and weight while the left and right wheels depreciate as a result of many high-speed right turns off the highway. Interchange them together with your spare tire after approximately every 7,500 miles of transit. This will reduce the number of times you'd need new tyres for your car.

102. Open windows at low speed and use air conditioner at high speed

Car air conditioners may consume up to 5% of fuel. So you can save gas by turning it off until you drive at high speed. At high speed open windows cause increased air resistance, forcing the engine to work harder to keep the wheels spinning. So it's windows at low speeds it's windows and air conditioning at high speeds.

103. Maintain tire pressure

Maintaining recommended tire pressures is not only safe, but also saves you money. In fact, it could save you about 3% on your gas bill because it takes more effort to turn an under-inflated wheel (imagine trying to ride a bike with a flat tire.)

104. Buying a used or reliable car is a smarter decision than leasing or paying loan on an expensive car

105. Travel in the off-season to save on airfare and other travel costs

106. Save on flights and hotels with travel points and rewards

A variety of credit cards offer points programs that allow you to earn points that you can use to pay for your travel expenses.

107. Choose safe, cheap but comfortable accommodations like hostels and campgrounds when you travel on a budget.

OTHER TIPS

108. Buying a big home may not be necessary yet

A house with 5 bedrooms and 4 bathrooms may not be necessary for two people. You could reassess a cheap house or find a roommate in a cheaper area. Don't spend more money than necessary for more rooms in an expensive neighbourhood, or find a roommate.

Although investing in a home is a great way to invest in your future, don't do it if you don't make enough money to cover your expenses.

109. Maintain a healthy "FOMO/YOLO" mindset.

The "you only live once" mentality and the "fear of missing out" phenomena that are so vividly portrayed on social media often mislead a lot of people. Although living in the moment is crucial, make sure you have checks and balances in place to stop you from saying yes to everything and overspending out of a fear of missing out.

110. Quit comparing your financial situation to other people's, particularly 'celebrities'

Desist from wasting money on unnecessary purchases in an attempt to impress people.

111. Make and customize your own beauty products with simple ingredients like coconut oil and essential oils.

112. Spend more time at home

It might not be pleasant, but you can make it enjoyable. Even with children, there is a ton of innovative ways to have fun at home.

If you're frequently invited out, practice saying no more often. You may even disclose to others, if you feel comfortable doing so, that you are living on a limited income and can no longer afford to go out on a regular basis.

113. Make your own cleaning supplies

You may already have ingredients for a natural all-purpose cleaner in your kitchen.

114. Use rechargeable batteries instead of disposable batteries

Rechargeable batteries have a higher initial cost, but they can be charged and used many times. Hence, you don't have to keep buying new batteries

115. Extract the last remnant of a product before discarding it

116. Utilize both sides of the paper and refill your ink cartridges.

117. Instead of purchasing software, use free software.

118. Add some water to shampoo and body wash without losing its usefulness

119. Each time you use that product, use a little less of it.

120. Explore do-it-yourself remedies
Gain fundamental DIY knowledge for fixing cars and homes. Online tutorials can be used to perform many repairs, which can save the

cost of hiring a professional. If it is safe to do so, investigate the problem first and see if you can fix it yourself before you hire a contractor.

121. Create DIY gifts for special occasions

Handmade gifts are often more sentimental than pricey ones from stores.

122. Take up sewing and make your own clothes

123. Swap or Exchange Services

Exchange services or skills with neighbours or friends. This could involve taking language classes, gardening, child care, or pet sitting.

124. Sell or give away items that you don't use but maintain with money.

(I'm sorry, but it could be your extra pet.)

125. Use your imagination to upcycle or recycle used   clothing or furniture

You can give things you already own new life and functions by transforming them.

126. Buy a set of hair clippers and cut men's hair at home

127. Use libraries instead of buying books and movies

128. Use safety razors instead of disposable razors

Safety razors are designed to last longer than disposable razors.

129. Replace disposable air filters with reusable ones.

Conclusion

The key to successful budgeting is finding strategies that work for you and align with your lifestyle and goals. Mix and match these creative approaches to create a personalized budgeting plan that you can stick to over the long term.

www.ingramcontent.com/pod-product-compliance
Lightning Source LLC
Chambersburg PA
CBHW071217290526
45796CB00008B/277